The Wine
Question
& Answer
Book

A Light-Hearted Guide

Helen M. Smith

The Oak Barrel Press
Miami, Florida

Published by The Oak Barrel Press
Copyright © 1998, by Helen M. Smith.
The Oak Barrel Press, 8770 Sunset Drive, Suite 262
Miami, Florida 33173

Printed in the United States of America

Library of Congress Catalog Card No.: 98-091724
ISBN: 0-9664046-0-2

Some of the images in this book were obtained from IMSI's
Master Clips Collection,1895 San Francisco Blvd. East,
San Rafael, California 94901-5506

Drawings by Teresa Marie Calluoni
Edited by June Rabin, Judith Alier, and Jane Richardson

Book design by
Thomas A. Williams & Co.
Coral Springs, Florida

Cover by
Suzanne Kuennen

Contents

Foreword

This book presents wine for the novice in an entertaining and concise manner. Readers may take advantage of the lively question-and-answer format to discover the pleasures of wine appreciation and to grasp a bit of wine's history. A little knowledge goes a long way toward enhancing the pleasure of sipping a glass of wine.

Helen Smith and her wine-tasting friends have for years tested their wine skills by quizzing each other during informal gatherings. They feel it has enhanced not only their wine knowledge, but their enjoyment of the wines served. Wine itself is known to add to the jovial camaraderie of the group.

—Professor Patrick (Chip) Cassidy
Florida International University

Acknowledgments

The author wishes to thank the following persons, all of whom shared their knowledge and encouraged me during the writing of this book. Bill Brotherton, Ralph (Red-Head) Blackwell, Dionisio Irizarry, Veronica Litton, David and Lin Ornstein, Rob and Lisa McCardle, Pamela Yeske, David and Dorann Truesdell, John Radencich, Robert Katims, Jimmy Weber, Constance Ryan and Tom Bales, Kevin and Kim Smith, Florence Green, and many others who contributed thoughts about what makes an easy-to-understand wine book.

Thanks also to my brother and his wife, Charles and Evelyn Smith, who gave me important feedback after reading the book's first draft.

Thanks to Chip Cassidy who, with patience and a sense of humor, first introduced me to the idea that wine education could be lively and entertaining. Chip is wine buyer for one of the largest wine dealers in the United States. A special thank-you to Steven Liebowitz, whose optimism was both encouraging and inspiring.

Introduction

Although people often tell me they wish they were more knowledgeable about wine and its pairing with food, they shy away from reading books on this subject. Despite excellent wine guides on the market, many feel that an evening spent with a glass of wine and wine literature would be confusing.

This guide is designed for just those people. Here is a short, casual source of basic wine information, or gain without pain. Use it as a self-challenging quiz, a game with friends, a reference, and an easy key to unlocking the secrets of wine wisdom and the pleasures of the grape. Let curiosity spark your spirit of adventure to guide you through the wine maze.

Sip one for me, Dear Reader.

Chapter 1

Wines of the World: A Bit of History

*Oh some are fond of Spanish wine,
and some are fond of French,
And some'll swallow tay and stuff fit
only for a wench.*
— John Masefield (1878-1967)

As you progress through this book, you will find a link between wine and history, politics, romance, the church, literature, the Bible, food, drama, and friendship. All of these characteristics contribute to wine's allure.

Wine, while not the filtered and refined drink available today, has been produced for perhaps 10,000 years. Yeasts in the environment, settling on fruits which then fermented with age, produced a naturally-occurring wine. Early humans enjoyed the delicious concoction and were no doubt inspired to create their own alcoholic beverages. Originally, wine was made from honey, dates, and other fruits. According to the Bible, Noah planted grape vines soon after departing the ark; surely his love of grape jelly did not motivate his agricultural habits.

In the time of England's Queen Elizabeth I (16th century), wines were so crude in texture and taste that they were fortified with ingredients such as honey, eggs, milk, cloves, aniseeds, camphor, and rice flour. This, we are told, improved the quality of these wines.

Increasingly, research, hard work, innovation, and tradition have transformed the wine industry, to our great benefit. Biologists, chemists, and other scientists—as well as computer specialists who record, document, and track winery statistics and other information—have contributed to the high quality of wines we enjoy today.

You do not need to purchase expensive bottles of wine. For everyday meals and gatherings, inexpensive jug wines are suitable. Bring a few bottles home from the store, sample them, and select a few that you and your family or friends enjoy. You can then keep a few bottles of those wines handy for yourself and for casual guests.

Many people enjoy only two or three wines and will drink only these wines. (Anyone is entitled to be an old poop.) Tastes differ. What one person considers unpleasant, others will find quite suitable.

However appreciated the wines you serve, the joy of being in the company of family and friends will be the highlight of any event.

Wine is earth's answer to the sun. —*Margaret Fuller*, in Lydia Maria Child, Letters from New York, 2nd series (1845).

Finally, an important note: Don't get hung up on correctness. Wine appreciation is not a science! For any food and circumstance more than one wine will be suitable. What was thought by the experts to be correct a century ago or even 50 years ago may be passé today; what is thought proper today may be passé years from now. Feel free to choose whatever you like.

Chapter 2

Questions & Answers

The Pleasures of Wine

Have fun with this question-and-answer section. Quiz your friends, test your own skills, or throw a casual party, stage a contest, and award the winner a bottle of wine.

It's always fun to drink a wine older than you. A unique gift is a bottle of wine whose vintage is the same as a birth date or an anniversary. Or purchase a bottle of Port for a birth or graduation gift, to be consumed at a special occasion in 10 or 20 years.

The last few chapters of this book contain reference material on food and wine, grapes, glasses, and bottles (directory found on the contents page) which may be useful tools as you look over the question-and-answer chapters.

Q. What is wine?
A. *Fermented (alcoholic) grape juice. Wines are also made from other fruits and even honey (a drink called mead).*

Viticulture is the science of grape growing.

From wine
what sudden
friendship
springs.
—*John Gay*

Only two of the
many grape
species make
respectable
wines: Vitis
vinifera, Vitis
labrusca; also
hybrids of the
two. Most wines
sold in stores
are made from
the Vitis vinifera
grapes.

Viniculture is the science of the making of wine. Whoop dee do!

Q. What are the different ways wines can be named?.

A. — *By region (Chablis, France)*
   — *By grape variety (Riesling)*
   — *By proprietary name (a winemaker's trademark) (Pacific Rim by Bonny Doon)*
   — *By the house where produced (Bollinger Champagne)*
   — *Generic (American Chablis and Burgundy)*
   — *Some wine labels read simply white or red table wine*

Q. Can a given grape make several styles of wine, even within a single winery?

A. *Yes. This can be bewildering when purchasing wines - but this book can help - refer to pages 85-103*

Q. Name the four common categories of wines seen in stores.

A. — *Table or still (a wine that is not effervescent)*
   — *Sparkling or Champagne*
   — *Fortified*
   — *Cooking wines. These are found only in grocery stores*

Q. Are supermarkets and other grocery stores "proper" wine dealers?

A. *You bet, and they have many wine bargains. They also save that extra trip to the wine shop.*

However, in some states and counties, laws prohibit the sale of wine in supermarkets.

Q. Are wines that require additional aging usually found in supermarkets?
A. *No.*

Q. Are wines that require additional aging found in gourmet and other specialty food markets?
A. *Yes, more and more, in states and counties that allow wine sales there.*

Q. May I go to a wine shop and feel comfortable asking a question such as, "I'm having dinner with friends who are serving beef stew. Can you suggest a wine under $7 to serve with that meal?"
A. *Absolutely. Reputable wine shop merchants are informed guides and will respect your price range. They can also teach you about wines, wine with food, and winemaking.*

Q. Is it permissible to sell and purchase wine by mail order and by the Internet?
A. *Yes, in some states. Look for web sites on the Internet. One company selling wines is Virtual Vineyards (http://www.virtualvin.com/). They will be happy to tell you whether or not they can ship wines to your area. There is controversy in some states regarding laws that prohibit sales through catalogs and the Internet.*

Q. Do most wine bottles now give information about the wine on the back label?
A. *Yes.*

Q. Why do some wines cost more than others?

A. *Here are a few of the items that may contribute to the high cost of some wines: wine grapes that are difficult to grow or must be harvested at a precise time; barrel or bottle aging of a wine; a vintage year or a low harvest yield; the size and location of the winery; the discretion of the bottler; the fame or rarity of the wine; advertising.*

Q. What denotes the quality of a fine wine?

A. *The balance of the wine's attributes: bright, clear color, pleasing aroma, substantial texture, a taste that is full of harmonious, complex flavors without harshness, and a pleasant aftertaste.*

Q. How do I know the wine in the bottle is worth the price?

A. *Comparison with other wines of the same region, grape, and year of harvest; taste-testing (is it worth the price to you?); word of mouth (do others you trust feel it is worth the price?); recommendations from a reputable wine dealer.*

Q. The year of the grape crop is often noted on the bottle. What is this called?

A. *Vintage. Vintage is often not important when purchasing a wine, unless you are buying an expensive barrel-aged wine or plan to age the wine yourself. Some years produce better grapes for wines; these vintage lists are available at many stores and in books.*

Q. Are most wines earmarked by wineries to be aged for several years?

A. *No. Only a small percentage, perhaps 10%, require aging.*

Listed below are some wines that may need aging after purchase, depending on the wine style, the year bottled, and the year purchased. These aged wines, both reds and whites, are generally more expensive than young wines.

— Cabernet Sauvignon (from many countries, including Bordeaux, France)

— Châteauneuf-du-Pape (French Rhône)

— Hermitage (French Rhône)

— Chianti Riserva (Italy)

— Barolo and Barbaresco (Italy)

— Pinot Noir (from many countries) and Burgundies (France)

— Riojas (Spain)

— Penedés (Spain)

— Shiraz (Australia)

— Vino Nobile di Montepulciano (Italy)

— Brunello di Montalcino (Italy)

— Chardonnays (from many countries)

— Some Ports

Everything is worth what its purchaser will pay for it.
—*Pubilius Syrus (First Century B.C.)*

Some countries or regions that may produce good wine bargains include:
— The Beaujolais area of France
— South Africa
— Chile and Argentina
— The United States
— Portugal
— Australia
— The Rioja area of Spain
— The Vin de Pays wines of France

Q. May wines that are spoiled upon opening be returned to the seller?

A. *Yes, but only if they were spoiled at the time of purchase. No fair cheating if your honey left the bottle in your hot car for three weeks.*

Q. Why do some wine bottles have screw tops and others have corks?

A. *Cork is the traditional seal for a wine bottle, dating back to a time when no other plug was tight enough. Today metal screw tops are found on some inexpensive wines and work just as well or better. Many people feel that, in time, all or most bottles will be sealed by screw tops.*

The term "corked" refers to wines that are spoiled, such as those caused by a contaminated cork.

Q. How do I get the cork pieces out of a bottle of opened wine?

A. *Short of purchasing a fancy cork remover, decant the wine into a larger-neck container and then remove the pieces as they float to the top, or pour the wine into individual glasses and remove the cork with a spoon. Or, why stand on ceremony, a deft finger can retrieve a cork piece quickly from your glass of wine without fuss.*

Q. Describe the wine from a corked bottle.

A. *There will be a musty or moldy chemical smell and taste (it has been described as smelling like wet cardboard).*

Q. Is smelling the cork from a wine bottle useful in deciding whether the wine inside is spoiled?

A. *No. Some movies, however, show restaurant scenes with patrons or servers smelling the corks. That's show biz.*

Q. Should wine bottles be stored out of the light?

A. *Yes, if you have room in your living quarters. If not, keep them away from windows or other light and heat. Improper storage (too much light or heat) can spoil the wine and it will taste corked. If you plan to drink your wines within a few weeks, storage is not as important.*

Q. Can an opened bottle of wine be saved for later use?

A. *Absolutely. There is a pump device (Vacu-Vin) on the market, with which, through a hole*

in its rubber stopper, air can be pumped from the bottle. The wine bottle can then be stored in a refrigerator. There are cans of inert gas on the market which squirt a cover of gas over the wine left in the bottle and protect it from coming in contact with air.

When dining out, it is acceptable and proper to ask your server for advice about the restaurant's wines. You don't have to be married to their advice.

Q. What is a sommelier?
A. *A wine server in a restaurant.*

Q. What would be important to check when first tasting a bottle of wine in a restaurant?
A. *Make sure the wine is what you ordered, and then check the color, aroma, and taste.*

Q. Name a single style of wine that everyone at an event would probably enjoy.
A. *Champagne. Don't the bubbles just make your nose tingle, eyes sparkle, and some noses turn red!*

Q. What is a wine taken before a meal called?
A. *Apéritif.*

Q. Is it proper to mix wine with other beverages (e.g., Champagne with juices)?
A. *Yes. You paid for the wine and you should feel free to enjoy it as you wish. At a gathering, however, others may like their wine without your diluting it.*

Q. Name a drink made by combining Cassis and white wine.
A. *Kir.*

Q. Name a drink made by combining Champagne and Cassis.
A. *Kir Royale.*

Q. Name a drink made by combining club soda and wine over ice.
A. *Spritzer. A pleasant drink with friends on a hot afternoon.*

Q. What is champagne mixed with orange juice called?
A. *Mimosa.*

Q. What is a crushed grape mixture to be made into wine called?
A. *Must (in English) and Mout (in French) . It is not called grape juice because it contains pulp, seeds, and skins.*

Q. What is a complex wine?
A. *One that has been aged before bottling. It will have more varied flavors than a simple wine.*

Q. What is replacing wooden barrels for storage in some wineries?
A. *Stainless steel tanks.*

Q. Is this storage as effective as traditional wooden containers?

Many people believe that the Chardonnay and Riesling grapes produce the greatest white wines in the world.

A. *Fine wines benefit from wooden barrel maturation and fermentation to promote flavor, clarity, and stability. Other wines do well in stainless steel.*

Q. What is the source of the woody flavor of some wines?
A. *Barrel aging. Some people enjoy a wine's woody flavor; others do not.*

If you can afford only one set of wine glasses, a first choice might be a 10 ounce clear wine glass. On the other hand, if you drink wine from a beer mug, the wine elf will not banish you to the wine cellar. Ha! You should be so lucky!

Q. How long should wines be chilled before drinking?
A. *For white wines, perhaps an hour, depending on individual preference; less time if it is a complex wine. Champagne may need a couple of hours in the refrigerator. Full-bodied red wines may need little chilling (about 65°); younger, lighter reds need more chilling. You're the one who is going to drink the wine, so experiment until it tastes right to you.*

Q. Name two terms for allowing wine to be exposed to the air before drinking.
A. *Breathing and aerating.*

Q. What effect can breathing have on an aged wine?

A. *It may taste smoother, after coming in contact with oxygen in the air. It is now felt that aged wines (including reds) should be poured directly into individual glasses so that each person may choose whether or not and how long to allow the wine to breathe in the glass before drinking.*

Q. Name the term for opening and pouring a bottle of wine into another container/wine glass.
A. *Decanting.*

Q. What wines always need to be decanted before being poured into glasses?
A. *Wines with sediment in the bottle, such as Vintage Ports. Proper decanting allows the sediment to remain in the bottle. When decanting a bottle of wine, hold it up to a light and pour it slowly into another container. By looking through the glass bottle with the light behind it, you can see the sediment pooling in the bottle neck and stop pouring before the sediment runs into the other container. Or, if you strain the wine through cheesecloth, who's to know?*

This is a good way to evaluate a wine:
- Look at color and clarity
- Swirl the wine in the glass to release the aroma
- Inhale and enjoy the aroma
- Taste the wine
- Savor the flavor and the aftertaste

It is possible, you know, to enjoy the wine by just drinking it, without all the folderol!

Q. What are "legs" or "tears" in the wine glass?
A. *Rivulets that coat and run down the inside of the glass after you swirl or sip the wine.*

Q. And what is a rivulet, for goodness sake?
A. *A streamlet of wine, like the contents running down the inside of a molasses bottle after it has been tilted.*

Q. How do we describe the taste of wine?
A. *By comparisons ("It tastes like" green apples, berries, almonds, et cetera).*

Q. What is the source of the astringent, mouth-puckering, dry sensation in some wines?
A. *Tannin (tannic acid).*

Q. Name a non-alcoholic beverage containing tannin.
A. *Tea.*

Q. What is a term used to describe a wine fuller than a full-bodied wine?
A. *Powerful or robust.*

Q. What does the term "body" of a wine refer to?
A. *The feel in the mouth (texture). And some have great bodies.*

Q. The term light wine can mean what three things?
A. *—Lower in calories.*
    —Less full-bodied, more sprightly.

—*Lower in alcohol.*
(No, it doesn't glow in the dark!)

Q. Which have a higher acid content, white wines or red wines?
A. *White wines.*

Q. What two factors determine the number of calories in wine?
A. *The alcohol content and the sugar content.*

Q. How many calories are there in a glass of table wine?
A. *90-110.*

At every gathering where wine is served, it is important that one person from each car . . .
Be a designated driver. In a pinch, spend the night with family or friends or take a taxi home.

Q. What percent of drunk driving arrests in the U.S. are caused by wine alone?
A. *Approximately two percent.*

Q. Which grapes grow best in northern climates: red or white?
A. *White grapes. Most wines are produced in the North and South Temperate Zones of the world.*

Q. If you were to open a winery, what two factors would be of utmost importance?
A. *Soil and climate. I wonder if the owners also check for the best view?*

Q. What is the name of an aphid that destroys grape vines by attacking the roots?
A. *Phylloxera.*

Q. The 1860s European Phylloxera catastrophe that killed many grape vines began on what continent?
A. *North America. Europe gave us its tired, its poor, its huddled masses yearning to breathe free; we sent it back a grape-vine killer.*

Q. What solved the 1860s Phylloxera infestation?
A. *The grafting of French grape vines onto American vine rootstocks.*

Europe in the 1860s was threatened with destruction of its wine industry by the Phylloxera infestation because wealthy families beautified their gardens by importing from America plants carrying the Phylloxera louse, which spread to grape vines. Today this aphid is affecting the United States, forcing wineries on the West Coast to tear out and replant their grape vines.

Q. What country is the biggest wine producer in the world?
A. *Italy. Does this surprise anyone?*

Q. What are the purposes of wine legislation enacted by most wine-producing countries?
A. *To ensure the consumer of quality control and for taxation purposes.*

Q. What are two disadvantages to strict government controls?
A. *Taxation increases the cost of wine, and controls may deter experimentation.*

Q. Name the U.S. federal agency that enforces wine legislation and regulation.
A. *The Bureau of Alcohol, Tobacco and Firearms. Remember them from Prohibition movies?*

Q. What English-speaking country consumes the most wine per capita?
A. *Australia. Is it any wonder they talk funny?*

Q. What is the French paradox?
A. *While the French smoke more cigarettes, eat more fatty foods, and exercise less than Americans, their rate of heart disease is lower than in the United States.*

Q. What is the reason for the French paradox?
A. *Possibly the moderate use of red wine (1-3 drinks of alcohol per day — less for women than for men — one drink being equal to four ounces of wine). Many restaurants pour wine glasses full, so one glass may be the equivalent of six or more ounces of wine.*

Q. What ingredient in red wine may contribute to the lower rate of heart attacks in the French?
A. *The phenolic compounds found in the skins, seeds, and stems of the grapes. Red grapes are higher in phenol than white grapes.*

Q. Mold on grapes can be as influential to wine as mold on cheese. Name some wines for which the *Botrytis cinerea* mold on the grape is essential.
A. *Sauternes and some dessert wines (late harvest wines).*

Q. What is another name for *Botrytis*?
A. *Noble mold. Or even noble rot. Give us a break!*

Q. Where in the world did winemaking originate?
A. *Georgia, the country in Eastern Europe, not our state.*

Q. What group is responsible for distributing grape vines throughout Europe?
A. *Romans. Where Roman roads went, and they coursed throughout the known world, the grape vines went also.*

Q. Who preserved winemaking during the Dark Ages?
A. *Monks, in their monasteries, for use in the Eucharist (communion).*

Q. When Shakespeare's Falstaff went to the Garter Inn, what was his wine of choice?
A. *Sack (sweetened Sherry).*

Most governmental legislative classifications of wines came about in the 20th century.

Wine Containers
The first use of the true glass wine bottles for wine storage was probably in the 18th century. The amphora was a large pottery bottle used for wine storage and for aging by the Greeks and Romans. But after the Middle Ages, the Europeans did not age wine until glass bottles and corks came into use.

Jug Wines

Q. Jug wines make up what percent of all U.S. wine sales?
A. *Approximately 50%, probably due to house wines poured from jugs in restaurants.*

Q. Name a large wine bottle, twice the size of the standard bottle.
A. *Magnum. Whoopee!*

Q. Are jug wines a good buy?
A. *Absolutely. The magnum bottles in particular are a bargain.*

Q. The jug wines in the U.S. labeled "light" have what percent fewer calories?
A. *Approximately 25%. This is good news for dieters, although the wines may taste weak.*

Q. What countries first sold wine in a disposable box (bag-in-a-box)?
A. *Australia and New Zealand. And it's great for picnics.*

Large jugs of wine often contain less than a gallon of wine, depending upon the state laws where purchased.

Some good magnums of wine:

L'Orval wines

Lindemans Sémillon Chardonnay

Ernest & Julio Gallo wines

Mondavi-Woodbridge wines

Vendange wines

Fetzer wines

August Sebastiani Hermitage wines

United States

I'm like old wine. They don't bring me out very often, but I'm well preserved.
—Rose Kennedy

Q. Does the U.S. consume more or less wine per capita than Italy?
A. *Less, by about an 8:1 ratio. We can't be #1 in everything.*

Q. What percent of wine sold in the U.S. is made in the United States?
A. *Approximately 75%.*

Q. Do only a few states produce wines?
A. *No. Many states have wineries, many of them*

Many famous European winemakers own land and wineries in the U.S.

30

sell wines locally. *The Valley Vineyards Winery in Morrow, Ohio, produces several styles of wine, runs a restaurant on the premises, hosts yearly wine festivals, and plans other activities for visitors.*

Q. Must all U.S. wines contain grapes from the winery or state where the wine is fermented?
A. *No. However, if state or vineyard names are found on the label, certain regulations do exist in some states.*

Q. In the U.S., what percent of the grapes used in a bottle of wine must be made from the grape named on the label?
A. *75 percent.*

Q. In Oregon, what percent of the wine in the bottle must be made from the grape named on the label?
A. *90 percent. These folks are serious about their wines.*

Q. In the last 20 years, have red or white wines become more popular in the U.S.?
A. *White wines, perhaps because we are eating more fish, white meats, pasta, and vegetables.*

Q. Name the four most productive wine states, starting with the highest volume wine producer.
A. *California, New York, Washington, and Oregon. Before the Civil War, Ohio was #1.*

Q. Approximately what percent of U.S. wines are made in California?
A. *90%.*

Q. What California area (Valley) produces the most wine?
A. *The San Joaquin Valley.*

Q. What California region is known for making the most full-bodied wines?
A. *Napa Valley.*

Q. Name two of California's most important universities involved in wine education and research.
A. *Fresno State and The University of California at Davis. A degree in booze — what a life!*

Q. What is the most heavily planted white grape in California?
A. *Colombard, a grape used most often as a blend.*

Q. What is the most heavily planted red grape in California?
A. *Zinfandel.*

Q. Zinfandel grapes make what styles of wines?
A. *Blush, red, and also late harvest wines; light-bodied, medium-bodied, and full-bodied wines.*

Q. Do both Oregon and Washington wineries produce medal-winning wines?
A. *Yes.*

Q. The famous wineries, Chateau Ste Michelle and Columbia Crest, are located in what state?
A. *Washington.*

Q. What is the major difference between the grape vines grown on the West Coast and many of those grown in the East and Midwest?
A. *West Coast grapes are from the* Vitis vinifera *species; further east, the* Vitis labrusca *grape species is commonly grown. Kosher wines in the Northeast are often made from the* Vitis labrusca *grape.*

Q. Name a term often used to describe the flavor and scent of many Vitis labrusca grapes.
A. *Foxy.*

Q. You mean it smells like the fur of an animal?
A. *Yes.*

> In the last few years, in the East, winemakers have planted more European grapes (*Vitis vinifera*) and hybrid grapes, producing what many believe are better wines than in the past.

The famous U.S. Zinfandel grape probably originated in Manduria, Italy. There, it is called "primitivo."

Q. What does "Reserve" on a wine bottle mean?
A. *Anything the winery wants it to mean, though it is usually a better wine.*

Q. Name four grapes that produce most of the late harvest dessert wines.
A. *Riesling, Gewürztraminer, Sémillon, and Sauvignon Blanc.*

Q. What important items would we look for on a U.S. bottle label?
A. *The winery/producer and the grape variety. Don't purchase a wine based on its flashy label, unless you are collecting labels.*

Q. Are late harvest wines bottled in magnums?
A. *No, usually in small bottles. They're pricey but delicious.*

Q. Gallo produces what percent of all wines sold in the U.S.?
A. *Approximately 25%.*

Q. What is a wine called that is made without pesticides or fertilizers?
A. *Organic wine.*

Q. What group brought Vitis vinifera grape vines from Mexico to California, starting the wine industry there in the 1700's?
A. *Franciscan missionaries.*

Q. What early U.S. President was known as a wine connoisseur who encouraged winemaking interests?
A. *Thomas Jefferson.*

Q. What famous 1920 U.S. government act wiped out many wineries?
A. *Prohibition. After repeal of that 18th amendment thirteen years later by the 21st amendment, it took the U.S. wine industry years to recover.*

Q. What President served the Robert Mondavi Cabernet Sauvignon in Paris?
A. *Richard Nixon.*

Q. In Beijing (Peking), what American sparkling wine was served to the Chinese?
A. *Schramsberg. The Chinese also make wine, but many factors limit their ability to produce the high-quality wines created in many other countries.*

Australia and New Zealand

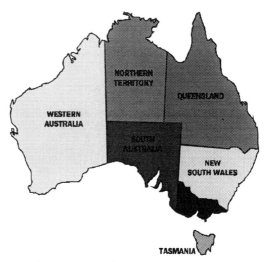

Q. What factors are felt to have contributed to an increase in the quality of wines from Australia?
A. *Both research and innovation, and also wine-tasting competitions. We, the consumers, are the winners in winery competitions and rivalries.*

Q. Most vineyards in Australia are located in what geographical area?
A. *Southeast. But other areas are expanding rapidly.*

Q. Name the four most important wine-growing states in Australia.
A. *New South Wales, Victoria, South Australia, and Tasmania.*

Q. Of these four areas, which produces the most wine?

A. *South Australia.*

Q. Do Australian wines tend to resemble European wines made from the same grape varieties?
A. *No. Many are less complex and have more fruity flavors.*

Q. Does each region make a limited style of wine, as in France?
A. *No. Many styles of wine are made, often in the same vineyard, as in the U.S.*

Q. What red grape is the most productive in Australia?
A. *Shiraz.*

A few of the many grape varieties grown in
Australia are listed below.
Shiraz
Pinot Blanc
Sauvignon Blanc
Cabernet Sauvignon
Grenache
Chardonnay
Sémillon
Merlot
Riesling
And there are some wine bargains here.

Q. What white grape is most productive in Australia?
A. *Chardonnay.*

Q. What is the most robust wine made in Australia?
A. *Shiraz. A powerful wine bursting with berry flavors.*

Q. Do Australian winemakers ever blend their grapes for making wines?
A. *Yes.They frequently blend, and their wine bottles may be labeled as such.*

Q. What important items would we look for on an Australian and New Zealand bottle label?
A. *Producer/winery and grape variety.*

Q. Does Australia ever label wines with proprietary names?
A. *Yes.*

Q. Australia sometimes calls its Sauvignon Blanc by what other name?
A. *Fumé Blanc.*

Q. Does Australia have strict wine laws?
A. *No. But they do control labeling requirements of finer wines.*

Q. The British settled Australia in 1788. When did they begin growing grapes for wine?
A. *That same year, 1788.*

The famous Coonawarra and Padthaway Districts and Barossa Valley are in South Australia.

Q. Does New Zealand produce mostly red or white wines?
A. *White wines.*

Q. In New Zealand, what are Marlborough, Hawks Bay, Auckland, and Gisborne?
A. *Regions. But they do sound like soccer players.*

Central and South America

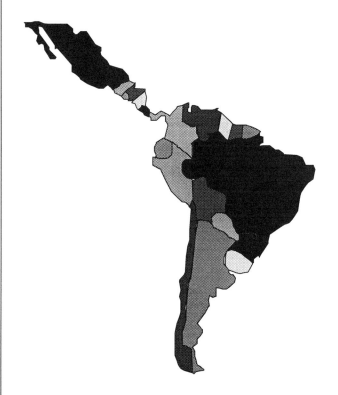

What though youth gave love and roses,
Age still leaves us friends and wine.
—Thomas Moore (1779-1852)

Q. Name the two major South American wine-producing countries.
A. *Chile and Argentina.*

Q. Which of the above is the fourth largest wine-producing country in the world?
A. *Argentina.*

Q. Have other countries invested in wineries in South America, as they have in the U.S.?
A. *Yes, including investments by U.S. companies.*

Q. Are Chile and Argentina famous for producing red wines, white wines, or both?
A. *Both red and white wines.*

Q. What do the terms Gran Reserva, Special, and Reservado on a Chilean wine label denote?
A. *The age of the wine. This age labeling is similar to that of the Rioja area of Spain.*

Q. Place the above terms in their proper order, starting with the least amount of aging.
A. *Special: aged at least two years.*
   Reservado: aged at least four years.
   Gran Reserva: aged at least six years.

Q. What important items would we look for on a Central and South American bottle label?
A. *Producer/shipper and grape variety.*

Q. What three geographical areas have kept the troublesome Phylloxera aphid out of Chile?
A. *The Andes Mountains to the East, the Atacama desert to the North, and the Pacific Ocean to the West.*

Q. What was the first country in the Americas to grow grapes for wine?
A. *Mexico.*

Wines of South Africa

There is always something new out of Africa.
—Pliny the Elder (A.D. 23-79)

Q. Why have we only recently begun to see South African wines in the U.S.?
A. *The U.S. boycott of South Africa was lifted only a few years ago.*

Q. Does South Africa make only a few styles of wine?
A. *No, it makes many styles of wine, as in the U.S.*

Q. What are South Africa's two most important wine-producing regions?
A. *Paarl and Stellenbosch.*

Q. Does South Africa produce many varieties of French grapes?
A. *Yes.*

Q. Name the famous South African grape that is a hybrid of the Pinot Noir and Cinsaut grapes.
A. *Pinotage.*

Q. And how did they get the term Pinotage from Pinot Noir and Cinsaut?
A. *The Africans call Cinsaut by the name Hermitage. Hence, "Pino tage" (pea no taj').*

Q. Describe the Pinotage wine.
A. *A dry red wine which requires barrel aging.*

Q. How are South African wineries usually organized?
A. *As cooperatives.*

Q. What important items would we look for on a South African bottle label?
A. *Grape variety and producer/commune.*

Q. Until recently, South Africa was best known in the U.S. for what style of wines?
A. *Sherry and other fortified wines.*

Germany

Forsake not an old friend; for the new is not comparable to him: a new friend is as new wine; when it is old, thou shalt drink it with pleasure.
—The Holy Bible: Apocrypha, Ecclesiasticus 9:10

Q. What are the four major German grape varieties?
A. *Riesling, Gewürztraminer, Sylvaner, and Müller-Thurgau.*

Q. Most German wines exported to the U.S. are from what area in Germany: North, South, East, or West?
A. *North.*

Q. How many legislative wine regions are there in Germany since Unification?
A. *Fourteen.*

Q. Name Germany's four major wine-producing regions.
A. *Mosel-Saar-Ruwer (the wines are often called Mosels), Rheingau, Rheinpfalz, and Rheinhessen (the wines are often called Rhines).*

Q. What is the distinction between the brown and green bottles of German wines?
A. *The Mosels are in green bottles, Rhines in brown bottles.*

Q. Which is a lighter, more delicate wine, Mosel or Rhine?
A. *Mosel.*

Q. Place in proper order these four classifications of wine, starting with the highest quality: Tafelwein, Landwein, QbA, and QmP.
A. *QmP, QbA, Landwein, Tafelwein.*

Q. Place these five styles of QmP (the highest quality wines) in proper order, starting with the first picked (driest): Beerenauslese, Auslese, Kabinett, Spätlese, and Trockenbeerenauslese.
A. *Kabinett, Spätlese, Auslese, Beerenauslese, Trockenbeerenauslese. What a mouthful!*

Liebfraumilch is a white German wine made chiefly for export.

Q. Are German wines usually sweet or dry?
A. *Sweet.*

Q. Are the drier wines or sweeter wines made from the earliest picked grapes?
A. *Drier.*

Q. What is the English translation of the German term Trocken on a wine bottle?
A. *Dry.*

Q. The Müller-Thurgau grape is a cross between the Sylvaner and what other grape?
A. *Riesling.*

Q. Name a wine produced from grapes picked partially frozen.
A. *Eiswein (ice wine).*

Q. What is the English translation of Liebfraumilch on a wine bottle?
A. *Milk of the blessed mother.*

Q. Chaptalization is the practice of adding sugar to the grape juice. Name the scientist and minister of Napoleon for whom this practice was named.
A. *Chaptal.*

Q. German law allows chaptalization for what purpose?
A. *To increase the alcohol content.*

Q. Are German sweet wines famous for their low or high alcohol content?
A. *Low. Usually 8-10%.*

Q. Are German wines usually served chilled or at room temperature?
A. *Chilled.*

Q.What important items would we look for on a German bottle label?
A. *Grape variety, region, sweetness, quality, and possibly vintage.*

Below are several items one might find on a German wine bottle label:

Region, vintage, village, quality, grape, style, shipper or producer, testing number, alcohol content, and possibly the estate where bottled. Whew!

Q. Are German grapes picked early or late?
A. *Late. The best wines come from grapes that are overripe.*

Q. What European leader in the 8th and 9th centuries was responsible for the proliferation of grape vines and winemaking throughout Germany?
A.*Charlemagne.*

Q. Isn't he the Emperor who brought the world out of the dark ages?
A. *Yes.*

Italy

Q. Name the five most important wine-producing regions in Italy.
A. *Veneto, Alto Adige, Piedmont, Emilia-Romagna, and Tuscany.*

Q. The Veneto wines are found near what famous city?
A. *Venice.*

Q. Name the three famous wines from the Veneto region in Northeast Italy.
A. *Soave (white) and Bardolino and Valpolicella (red).*

Q. Describe the above three wines from the Veneto region.
A. *Light-bodied and casual.*

The term *Classico* on a bottle label of Soave, Bardolino, or Valpolicella may indicate a better wine than a bottle without this term on the label.

Q. Name the Emilia-Romagna region wine that is one of the best selling wines in the U.S.
A. *Lambrusco.*

Q. Describe Lambrusco wines.
A. *Low in alcohol, slightly effervescent, dry or sweet, and light-bodied.*

Q. Name three important red grapes from the Piedmont region.
A. *Nebbiolo, Barbera, and Dolcetto.*

Q. Of these three wines, which two are named for the grape variety: Barbera, Dolcetto, and Chianti?
A. *Barbera and Dolcetto.*

Q. The Dolcetto wine has a style resembling what French wine?
A. *Beaujolais. Fruity and light-bodied.*

The Nebbiolo grape is responsible for these three wines: Barolo, Barbaresco and Gattinara.

Below are four Piedmont wines, listed in descending order of complexity:

Barolo

Barbaresco

Barbera and Dolcetto.

Q. What is the major central wine region in Italy?
A. *Tuscany.*

Q. For which red wine is Tuscany famous?
A. *Chianti.*

Q. What is the major grape used for Chianti?
A. *Sangiovese.*

Q. Place these three Chiantis in descending order of quality: Chianti Classico Reserva, Chianti Classico, Chianti.
A. *Chianti Classico Reserva, Chianti Classico, Chianti.*

Q. The picture of what animal appears on the seal of many Classico Chianti bottles?
A. *Rooster.*

Q. What are Chianti bottles in straw called?

A. *Fiaschi. These bottles of wine taste thin and nothing like the rich, tannin, berry or cherry-tasting, aged Chiantis found in Bordeaux-like bottles, often great bargains.*

Q. What are two other famous quality red wines from Tuscany?
A. *Brunello di Montalcino and Vino Nobile di Montepulciano. These are expensive, bold, and some of Italy's best.*

Q. Should the two wines named above be consumed young?
A. *No. These are wines meant for aging.*

Q. What important items would we look for on an Italian bottle label?
A. *Producer, region, grape or style.*

Spain and Portugal

Q. What is the Spanish name for winery or cellar?

A. *Bodega.*

Q. Why have Spanish wines become more popular in the U.S. in recent years?

A. *The high prices of French wines forced retailers to look elsewhere for fine wines.*

Q. Name three important wine-producing areas of Spain.

A. *Rioja, Sherry (Jerez), and Catalonia. Sherry will be covered under fortified wines.*

Q. Are most Rioja wines sold in the U.S. red or white?

A. *Red.*

Four important red grapes used in the Rioja region are Garnacha, Tempranillo, Graciano, and Mazuelo. An important white grape is the Viura (Macabeo).

Q. Describe most famous Rioja red wines.
A. *Bordeaux-like, oaky, buttery, and dry.*

Q. The winemakers of what country came to the Rioja area of Spain in the 19th century to escape the Phylloxera infestation?
A. *Bordeaux, France. Many Rioja wines today still resemble the Bordeaux wines of that time.*

> Rioja wines are often labeled in the following way to denote years of aging required before sale. Wineries may, however, age them for longer periods.
> Gran Reserva: 5 years (2 in barrel and 3 in bottle).
> Reserva: 3 years (1 in barrel and 2 in bottle).
> Crianza: 2 years (1 in barrel and 1 in bottle)

Q. The new Penedès wines are being made from grapes made famous in what country?
A. *France.*

Q. What famous wine-growing family name is linked to the Catalonia region of Penedès?
A. *Torres.*

Q. What important items would we look for on a Spanish bottle label?
A. *Bodega/producer, proprietary name, and style.*

Q. Does Portugal export much wine except for Port and Madeira?
A. *Yes. Lots of wine bargains here also.*

Q. What is perhaps the best Portuguese still wine region?
A. *Dão.*

Q. What two famous, slightly effervescent wines does Portugal produce?
A. *Mateus and Lancers.*

Q. What is the famous green wine of Portugal?
A. *Vinho Verde, a dry, fresh wine—usually white—a bit effervescent.*

Q. What important items would we look for on a Portuguese bottle label?
A. *Bodega, proprietary name, and region.*

France

We're now into the hoity-toity stuff. If you want to be a wine snob, you need to know this country's wines.

Q. What are the geographic wine-growing areas of France called?
A. *Appellations.*

Q. Name the six famous French wine appellations.
A. *Alsace, Bordeaux, Burgundy, Champagne, Loire Valley, and Rhône.*

Q. Name the one French appellation where wines are named for grapes, as in the U.S.
A. *Alsace.*

Q. May individual French appellations produce un-limited wines and styles, as in the U.S.?
A. *No. In France, government legislation limits many factors of winemaking.*

Q. Place these French wines in descending order of quality: Appellation d' Origine Contrôlée (A.O.C.), Vin de Table, Vin de Pays, Vin Délimité de Qualité Supérieure (V.D.Q.S.)
A. *Appellation d'Origine Contrôlée, Vin Délimité de Qualité Supérieure, Vin de Pays, and Vin de Table.*

Q. What is the most common grape grown in France?
A. *Carignan. This is often used as a blend with other grapes, but you may never see its name on a wine bottle label.*

Q. What is the meaning of the French term *"Cru?"*
A. *Growth, but translates into vineyard or commune, as in Grand Cru (great growth).*

Q. What is a term meaning "Bottled by the owner at the château"?
A. *Estate bottled.*

Q. What famous French scientist in the 1800s researched the fermentation process?
A. *Pasteur. (Pasteurization takes its name from this scientist.)*

Alsace

Important grapes grown in Alsace include: Riesling, Sylvaner, Pinot Blanc, Pinot Gris (Tokay), Gewürztraminer, Muscat, Pinot Noir, and Chasselas.

Q. Does Alsace produce mostly white or red wines?
A. *White.*

Q. Similar grapes are grown in Alsace and Germany; name some of the differences in the wines produced.
A. *Alsatian wines are more full-bodied, higher in alcohol, drier, and a bit spicy.*

Q. Which of the Alsatian grapes makes a spicy, aromatic dry wine, as well as a sweet dessert wine?
A. *Gewürztraminer. Gesundheit.*

Q. What important items would we look for on an Alsatian bottle label?
A. *The grape variety and producer/shipper.*

Q. During the years between the Franco-Prussian War and World War I, Alsace found itself under the rule of what country which forced it not only to change its wine styles, but also to produce less wine?
A. *Germany.*

Shippers who buy grapes, crushed grape juice, or wines from growers and then produce wines for final sale are called négociants.

Bordeaux

Many wine lovers consider Bordeaux the producer of the best wines in the world. A love of these wines is a taste that develops slowly.

Q. What are the two categories of wine quality in Bordeaux, starting with the highest quality?
A. *Château and regional. Château wines will give the name of the Château on the label. Regional wines will give the name of the region where the wine was made.*

Q. What important items would we look for on a Bordeaux bottle label?
A. *Château, vintage, and appellation.*

<u>White Bordeaux</u>
Q. Name the four major white Bordeaux areas.
A. *Graves, Sauternes, Barsac, and Entre-Deux-Mers.*

Q. Does the Graves region produce only white wines?
A. *No. But it is most famous for its whites.*

Q. The white, dry Graves wines are made from what three grapes?
A. *Sauvignon Blanc, Sémillon, and Muscadelle.*

Q. Should white Graves wines, aged in oak with vanilla and oaky flavors, always be served with food?
A. *No. They are also delicious by themselves, for sipping.*

Entre-Deux-Mers produces both wines labeled Bordeaux AC (red wine) and wines labeled Entre-Deux-Mers (dry white).

Sauternes are produced only in the Sauternes region of France. Other countries often produce sweet or semi-sweet wines which are sometimes called Sauterne.

Q. The white, sweet Sauternes wines are made from what three grapes?
A. *Sémillon, Sauvignon Blanc, and Muscadelle. These grapes also produce Graves wines, but the style of wine is different.*

Q. Are Sauternes grapes picked late or early in the season?
A. *Late in the season.*

Q. What, by law, is the minimum alcohol content of Sauternes?
A. *13%.*

Q. Are Sauternes served warm or cold?
A. *Cold.*

Q. What are common names for wines made in the Sauternes style in the U.S. and elsewhere?
A. *Late harvest wines or dessert wines (although Sauternes are also served as an apéritif or during a meal).*

Because Sauternes are wines made after the grape has been infected with the Botrytis mold and since their production can be a precarious endeavor, Sauternes are expensive.

Q. Is Barsac a dry wine or a sweet wine?
A. *Sweet.*

Red Bordeaux

I rather like bad wine....One gets so bored with good wine.
—Benjamin Disraeli, from the novel *Sybil.*
(A good quote for a wine snob.)

Q. What is a British name for red Bordeaux?
A. *Claret.*

Q. What was Claret called in the reign of Elizabeth I of England?
A. *Gascoigne or Galloway.*

Q. Name the three major grapes used for making the full-bodied red Bordeaux wines.
A. *Merlot, Cabernet Sauvignon, and Cabernet Franc.*

Q. What are reasons for blending grapes such as Merlot and Cabernet Franc with Cabernet Sauvignon?
A. *To soften the wines and for balance.*

Q. Name four main red wine regions of Bordeaux.
A. *Médoc, Pomerol, St. Emilion, Graves.*

Q. Of these last four regions, many consider two to be the most important, producing the finest wines. Name them.

A. *Médoc and Pomerol.*

Q. The Médoc area has four significant appellations within its borders. Name them.
A. *Margaux, Pauillac, St-Estéphe, and St-Julien.*

Q. How many châteaux are there in Bordeaux?
A. *Thousands, but many are ranked according to quality (classification), with the top five of the Grands Crus Classés being called Premiers Crus Classés.*

Q. Name the five Premiers Crus Classés (the five best red Bordeaux wines).
A. *Château Lafite-Rothschild, Château Latour, Château Margaux, Château Haut-Brion, and Château Mouton-Rothschild.*

Q. When and by whom were these châteaux classified?
A. *In 1855, by the Bordeaux wine industry.*

> ### *What is a vintage chart?*
>
> A list of the wine vintages (years of harvest), describing exceptionally good years. The wines from these years are usually more expensive than those from non-vintage years.

Burgundy

Q. In Burgundy, what does the term *Côte* mean?
A. *Hill or slope.*

Q. How many regions are there in Burgundy?
A. *Six.*

Q. Name the Burgundy regions.
A. *Chablis, Côte d'Or (Côte de Nuits, and Côte de Beaune), Côte Chalonnaise, Mâconnais, and Beaujolais.*

Q. Name the famous Burgundy grape varieties.
A. *Pinot Noir, Gamay, Chardonnay, Aligoté, and Pinot Blanc.*

The following are the three classifications of Burgundy wines, listed in order of descending quality: Grand Cru , Premier Cru, and Village Cru.

Red Burgandy

Q. Describe Beaujolais wines.
A. *Red, fruity, light-bodied, and fresh.*

Q. Name the only grape used for making Beaujolais wines.
A. *Gamay.*

64

Q. Place the following three Beaujolais in descending order of quality: Beaujolais Villages, Beaujolais, Cru Classé Beaujolais

A. *Cru Classé Beaujolais, Beaujolais Villages, Beaujolais.*

Q. Name the 10 famous Cru Classé Beaujolais Villages.

A. *Brouilly, Chénas, Chiroubles, Côte de Brouilly, Fleurie, Juliénas, Morgon, Moulin-à-Vent, Régnié, and Saint-Amour. Their names will appear on the bottle labels.*

Q. Name the newly fermented, bottled Beaujolais, meant to be enjoyed sooner rather than later (not to exceed six months from the date of release).

A. *Beaujolais nouveau.*

Q. In what month is this new Beaujolais released each year?
A. *November. Wine dealers consider this the beginning of their holiday season.*

Q. What is the major grape used for making Burgundy red wines?
A. *Pinot Noir.*

Q. Describe Pinot Noir Burgundy wines.
A. *Light and fruity, or full-bodied, and soft with long aging.*

Q. Place the following five Burgundy categories in descending order of quality. Commune, grand cru, region, district, and premier cru.
A. *Grand cru, premier cru, commune, district, and then region.*

Q. What important items would we look for on a Burgundy bottle label?
A. *Appellation, vintage, and producer/shipper or estate.*

White Burgundy
Q. What famous grape is used to make almost all white Burgundies?
A. *Chardonnay.*

The Côte d'Or, Beaujolais, Côte Chalonnaise, and Mâconnais are famous red wine regions.

Q. Besides Chardonnay, what other white grapes are used to produce Burgundies?
A. *Pinot Blanc and Aligoté.*

Q. Name the four white wine Burgundy regions.
A. *Chablis, Maconnais, Côte de Beaune, and Côte Challonaise.*

Q. What Burgundy region produces only dry wines from the Chardonnay grape?
A. *Chablis.*

Many wine lovers feel that Côte de Beaune produces the greatest white wines in the world.

Q. How many classifications are there for French Chablis?
A. *Three.*

Q. Is the lowest classification, Chablis, (not a Grand Cru Chablis or Premier Cru Chablis classification) often a good buy?
A. *Yes.*

Here are three ways the Chablis wines of France may differ from Chablis wines produced in other countries: Chablis are made only in the Chablis area of France (other countries use the name generically), French Chablis are always dry, and always made from the Chardonnay grape.

Q. Many Côte de Beaune Burgundies have on their label the name of a hospital. Name it.
A. *The Hospices de Beaune.*

Q. Did chaptalization (addition of sugar to the juice) originate in France (Burgundy) or in Germany?
A. *Burgundy.*

Rhône

Q. Describe most Rhône wines.
A. *Red, dry, full-bodied.*

Q. What grape is most important in the northern Rhône region?
A. *Syrah (the same grape as the Shiraz in Australia).*

Q. Name the three famous red wines from the north.
A. *Hermitage, Côte Rôtie, and Crozes-Hermitage.*

Q. Name the most important grape used for wines in the Southern Rhône region.
A. *Grenache.*

Q. Name the famous red wine from the South.
A. *Châteauneuf-du-Pape. Châteauneuf-du-Pape is made from a blend of grapes, including Grenache, Syrah, and Cinsault.*

Q. Name one of the most famous rosé wines in the world, from the Southern Rhône region.
A. *Tavel.*

Q. Name two ways Tavel wine differs from most U.S. rosés.
A. *It is generally drier and more full-bodied.*

Q. Is the Lirac wine a red or a white wine?
A. *It can be red, rosé, or white. It is always dry.*

Q. Are Rhône wines sold by négociants or by individual growers?
A. *Both.*

Q. The Catholic Church moved its papal court to the Rhône Valley in what century?
A. *Fourteenth Century.*

Q. What is the English meaning of the term Châteauneuf-du-Pape?
A. *New House of the Pope.*

Q. What important items would we look for on a Rhône wine label?
A. *Producer/Shipper or estate, vintage, and appellation.*

The Côtes du Rhône wine is a good bargain from the Rhône region.

Q. Name a famous white wine from the Rhône region.
A. *Condrieu, made from the Viognier grape.*

Loire Valley
Q. Name the three most important grapes in this region.
A. *Chenin Blanc, Sauvignon Blanc, and Muscadet (Melon). Don't expect the latter to taste like melon.*

Q. Are most Loire Valley wines red or white?
A. *White.*

Q. Name the five famous wines from the Loire region.

A. *Muscadet, Vouvray, Sancerre, Pouilly-Fumé, and Anjou Rosé.*

Q. What important items would we look for on a Loire Valley bottle label?
A. *Vintage and appellation.*

Loire Valley wines are generally light-bodied, dry, and cooling.

Champagne

A true German can't stand the French, Yet willingly he drinks their wines.
—Goethe (1749-1832)

The only country to make champagne is France. In the United States a "sparkling wine" can be the equivalent of champagne, but it is not from France.

Q. What are the two major differences between the making of still wine and the making of champagne?
A. *Champagne is fermented not once but twice, and it holds in the bottle the carbon dioxide given off during the second fermentation, hence, its effervescence upon opening. Pop the cork!*

Q. Name the method used in the making of champagne.
A. *Méthode champenoise, or traditional method.*

Q. What type of container is used for champagne's first fermentation?
A. *Either wood or stainless steel.*

Q. In what vessels does the second fermentation of the grape juice take place?
A. *Bottles.*

Q What is the term for allowing a wine to remain in contact with the coarse sediment?
A. *Sur Lie. The purpose of this practice is to enhance the flavor of the wine.*

Because Champagne is under bottle pressure, the bottle should be opened slowly, holding onto the cork, and with the bottle neck pointed away from people, valuables, and breakable items.

Q. For what are Champagne wines named?
A. *The Houses where they are produced, such as House of Bollinger.*

Q. Name the three famous grape varieties used for making champagne.
A. *Chardonnay, Pinot Meunier, and Pinot Noir.*

Q. Name a few of the many champagne varieties found in shops that sell wine.
A. *Blanc de Blanc, Rosé, Cuvée reserve bottling, Blanc de Noir, brut, very dry, sec, demi-sec, doux, and crémant.*

Q. The above varieties can exist in what form?
A. *Vintage and non-vintage*

Q. Blanc de Blanc champagne is made from what grape?
A. *Chardonnay.*

Q. Name the two grapes that can be used for making Blanc de Noir.
A. *Pinot Noir and Pinot Meunier.*

The term cuvée means a blend of grapes; cuvée reserve or speciale on a bottle of Champagne usually denotes a higher quality wine.

Q. Which is drier, Brut or Extra Dry Champagne?
A. *Brut.*

Q. What is a crémant Champagne?
A. *One that has only moderate effervescence or sparkle.*

Q. Name some Champagnes that would pair well with desserts.

A. *Sec, Demi Sec, and Doux. These are sweet or semi-dry Champagnes.*

Q. What shape glasses should be used for Champagne, and why?
A. *Tulip or flute-shaped (tall and thin), so the bubbles do not readily escape.*

Q. Can most Champagnes be aged for 10 or 15 years after purchase?
A. *No. Most are ready for consumption upon purchase and should be consumed within a couple of years at most.*

Q. What important items would we look for on a Champagne bottle label?
A. *Producer, style, and possibly vintage.*

Q. What famous Champagne is named for the 17th century Benedictine monk who used heavy bottles to prevent breakage and developed the art of making Champagne bubbly?
A. *Dom Pérignon.*

Q. Many of the wine cellars in the Champagne region were originally chalk mines. Who created these mines?
A. *The Romans.*

Q. What percent of vineyards in Champagne are owned by the Champagne producers?
A. *Approximately 8%.*

Sparkling Wines and Other Wines

Many countries of the world use the Méthode Champenoise for making sparkling wines.

Sparkling Wines

Q. Name a method of making quality sparkling wine that is less expensive than the Méthode Champenoise.

A. *Charmat. The Charmat process of making sparkling wine allows fermentation to take place in a tank, under pressure, rather than in bottles, after which the wine is bottled. This is a faster and cheaper than the méthode champenoise.*

Q. Henkell and Deinhard are two of the most famous sparkling wines sold in the U.S. from what country?

A. *Germany.*

Q. Freixenet and Codorníu are two sparkling wines imported to the U.S. from what country?
A. *Spain. Another name for a Spanish sparkling wine is Cava.*

Q. Cinzano Brut, Ferrari, Trentino, Prosecco, and Asti Spumante are sparkling wines imported from what country?
A. *Italy.*

Other Wines

Q. Name several other countries producing quality wines.
A. *Hungary, Bulgaria, Austria, Switzerland, Romania, Israel, and Canada.*

Q. What is one of the most modern winemaking countries of Eastern Europe?
A. *Bulgaria. Bulgaria is a quality wine producing country, in part because the former Soviet Union supplied funds to it as an agricultural nation whose activities included grape growing and winemaking.*

Q. What is Retsina?
A. *A wine flavored with pine sap or resin.*

Q. What country is famous for producing Retsina?
A. *Greece.*

Q. Wines imported from what country are kosher?
A. Israel.

Q. The famous dessert Tokay wine is from what country?
A. *Hungary.*

Q. Why are Canadian wines limited in production?
A. *The cold climate limits grape growing.*

Q. Like wines from many midwestern and southern states, English wines are usually available only in what area?
A. *Locally.*

Fortified Wines

Claret is the liquor for boys; port for men; but he who aspires to be a hero must drink brandy.
—Samuel Johnson (1709-1784)

Q. What is a fortified wine?
A. *One with an added neutral spirit, such as brandy.*

Q. What was probably the first fortified wine produced?
A. *Sherry.*

Q. Sherry is made in what country?
A. *Spain.*

Q. For what is Sherry named?
A. *A city, Jerez de la Frontera, Spain.*

Q. What are the two most important grape varieties used in the making of Sherry?
A. *Palomino and Pedro Ximenez.*

Q. What is the difference between the Fino and the Oloroso Sherries?
A. *The Fino Sherries—Fino, Manzanilla, and Amontillado—are dry and pale. The Oloroso Sherries—Oloroso, Pale Cream, and Cream— are higher in alcohol, less biting, darker, and may be sweetened.*

Q. Which of the above Sherries is the sweetest?
A. *Cream.*

Q. Which of the above Sherries is the most popular in the U.S.?
A. *Cream.*

Q. Dry Sherries are served at what temperature?
A. *Chilled.*

Q. Sherry is particularly popular in what English-speaking country?
A. *England.*

Q. Port comes from what country?
A. *Portugal.*

Q. Why does Port need decanting and Sherry does not?
A. *Many old Ports develop a sediment in the bottle.*

Below are descriptions of four ports:
Tawny: Wine aged in wood 6-8 years before bottling.
Ruby: Wine from several different years which has aged two or three years.
Aged Tawny: Wine aged in wood 10-20 years or more before bottling, is light in color. The label will show the age in years.
Vintage: Wine from the best grapes grown in the best year, aged in wood 2 years, then aged in bottle for many, many years.

We should look for the style, producer, and possibly the grape variety on a Sherry bottle.

Q. Which of the above four Ports tastes fruitier and sweeter?
A. *Ruby.*

Q. Which of the above four Ports is generally the least expensive, and which is the most expensive?
A. *Least expensive: Ruby. Most expensive: Vintage.*

Q. At what temperature should Port be served?
A. At room temperature.

Q. Although Port is produced in Oporto, Portugal, what country is largely responsible for its creation at the end of the 18th century?
A. *England.*

Q. What is the purpose of white paint on some vintage Port bottles?
A. *It is there so that if a bottle is moved to another bin, the same side can be placed facing up.*

The French, unlike the British and Americans, drink Port as an apéritif.

Q. Name a Portuguese island that makes another famous fortified wine.
A. *Madeira.*

Q. The *estufa* method of making Madeira is a heating of the wine. In what traveling vessel was this method of heating Madeira accidentally discovered while transporting fortified wine?
A. *Ships sailing to the East Indies and the Americas.*

Q. Is Vermouth a fortified wine?
A. *Yes.*

The practice of blending must from different years in tiers of barrels for the making of fortified wines is called the *solera* system.

Q. Which is sweeter, Port or Sherry?
A. *Port is usually the sweeter wine.*

Q. What is the purpose of the *solera* system?
A. *It keeps the style of the wine consistent year after year.*

Q. What kitchen condiment may be made by the *solera* system?

A. *Some better vinegars. This will sometimes be mentioned on the bottle label.*

Q. What was the most popular wine among the American colonists?
A. *Madeira.*

Now a question for all you beer lovers.

Q. *Who discovered bottled, effervescent-style ale and beer, and when?*
A. Dr. Alexander Nowell, Dean of St. Paul's Cathedral during the reign of Queen Elizabeth I of England. He was an avid fisherman, who left his tightly-corked beer container lying in the wet, cool grass one day while fishing. When he returned, he discovered the beer was a delightful, effervescent drink, much improved from the usual fare. And so, bottled beer became the popular drink it is today.

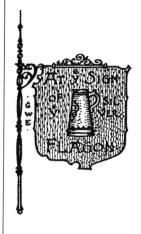

Brace yourself. There's more!

"I love thee, next to Malmsey in the morning, of all things transitory."
—John Fletcher
(1579-1625)

81

Chapter 3

Wine Basics

What to Look for on Wine Labels, Country by Country

Check the wine label items listed below, and learn to identify good buys based on your wine tastes and price range. If you find a wine you enjoy, memorize or write down the items necessary to identify it so that you may purchase the wine again.

United States
Grape variety and winery/producer

Australia and New Zealand
Grape variety and winery/producer

Central and South America
Grape variety and producer/shipper

South Africa
Grape variety and producer/commune

Germany
Grape variety, region, sweetness, quality, and possibly vintage

Italy
Producer, region, grape, or style

Spain
Bodega/producer, proprietary name, and style

Portugal
Bodega, proprietary name, and region

France
Alsace: Grape variety and producer/shipper
Bordeaux: Château, vintage, and appellation
Burgundy: Vintage, producer/shipper or
estate, and appellation
Rhône: Producer/shipper or estate, vintage,
and appellation
Loire: Vintage and appellation
Champagne: Producer, style, and possibly
vintage

Sherry
Producer, style, and possibly grape variety

Port
Producer, vintage, and style

How to Identify Wine Bottles and Wine Glasses

Wine glasses and bottles can be identified by their sizes and shapes.

As you can see below, the bottles are named for the old country wines and regions. However, all countries use these same bottle shapes, which denote similar wine styles.

Bordeaux-Style   Burgundy-Style

German-Style   Champagne-Style

Wine can be enjoyed from any glass, but the wine's flavors and characteristics are enhanced with certain style glasses. Below are the more popular glasses.

Champagne   White Wine

Red Wine   Brandy

Wine Styles

The phrase "wine style" refers to how the wines feel and taste in the mouth. Taste-testing wine is important when deciding what you like and what to buy. There is a greater assortment of wine styles than the grapes from which they are made because wine character is not defined by the grape alone.

85

Also contributing to the wine's style are, among other things, country of origin, soil and moisture in the area where the grapes are grown, age of the grape vine, mixture of grape must which makes up the wine, length of time the grape must is allowed to stay in contact with the skins, preferences of the winery's owner and winemaker, and amount and vessel of aging.

Texture

Texture is one component of wine style (other components, such as color, flavor, and aging are covered in the question and answer section). Texture describes how wine feels in the mouth. For example, a *light-bodied* wine might be compared to skim milk, light in the mouth; a *medium-bodied* wine feels a little fuller in the mouth, like 2% fat milk; and a *full-bodied* wine feels fuller-bodied yet, like whole milk. A *robust* wine is one that is even more powerful than a full-bodied wine. Wines described as soft feel smooth (like chocolate mousse) in the mouth.

Here's an example of the variations of wines that can be made from one grape: Chardonnay grapes make light wines for sipping or barrel-aged wines that are full-bodied. The wines are called white Burgundy in France or simply Chardonnay in Australia and the United States. They also are used for some of the white Champagnes of France and the sparkling wines of the United States and other countries. Wine made from Chardonnay grapes can be inexpensive if not aged or expensive if aged.

Rosé and Blush Wines (usually light-bodied)

The term *blush wine* was coined by American wine producers in the 1970s. Blush and *rosé* are different names for the same style of wine. These wines are made from red grapes, but the juice is allowed to remain with the grape skins for such a short time that only a touch of color is added to the must. These wines can be either dry or medium sweet, and, particularly in the United States, are light-bodied, although there are rosés with body.

Tavel wine from the Rhône region of France is a dry rosé wine. White Zinfandel is a slightly sweet blush wine.

White Wines
Light-Bodied

These are wines without aging, usually inexpensive, including jug wines. Drink chilled. These make good sipping wines. A good sipping wine is a wine that is pleasant without food. This does not mean that it cannot be consumed at a meal as well.

Some examples are Soave, young Chardonnay, Sauvignon Blanc, Chenin Blanc, Pinot Gris (Pinot Grigio), Sémillon/Chardonnay, Sylvaner, Pinot Blanc, Sémillon, and Muscadet.

Aromatic Wines

Wines with a flowery scent (spicy scent for Gewürztraminer) make a dry, medium, or sweet (dessert) wine. These are also good sipping wines.

Some examples are Gewürztraminer and Riesling.

Full-Bodied Wines
   Wines aged in barrels before bottling. More expensive than light wines. Best served a tad less chilled than light-bodied wines to bring out the complexity of the flavors. Generally meant to be consumed with food. Some examples are Chardonnay (including Burgundy), Graves (Sémillon/Sauvignon Blanc), Sémillon/ Chardonnay from Australia, Pinot Gris, Riesling, and Chenin Blanc.

Red Wines
Light-Bodied
   Can be consumed cold, even over ice. Often inexpensive. Good sipping wines. Some of these are fruity, such as Beaujolais. Some examples are Gamay (including Beaujolais), young Zinfandel, Dolcetto, Bardolino, Valpolicella, some Rhône, Lambrusco, and many jug wines (unaged, simple wines, found in any size bottle).

Medium-Bodied
   Sometimes aged in barrel before bottling. Served slightly chilled. Some examples are Merlot, some Zinfandel, Rioja, Pinot Noir (including Burgundy), some Barbaresco, some Chianti, and light Cabernet Sauvignon wines.

Full-Bodied
Some of the great wines of the world. Sometimes aged and expensive. Best served at about

65° (room temperature in old castles). Some examples are Cabernet Sauvignon and Merlot (including Bordeaux), Shiraz, some Chianti, some Zinfandel, Barolo, some Northern Rhône, Syrah, some Barbaresco, Sangiovese (Chianti Classico), and some Grenache wines.

A trusted wine merchant can help you sort through the different wine styles.

Chapter 4

The Great Grapes and Their Affinities, and Specialty Wines

White Grapes

Chardonnay
<u>Description</u>
A golden grape which makes white wines that are among the most popular and finest in the world. Can produce dry, bold, full-bodied wines. Creates wines that can be consumed young or aged for complexity, with flavors of oak, vanilla, butter, fruit, and nuts. This grape is also used in the making of Champagne and Sparkling Wine.

<u>Native Country</u>
France. It may be labeled Chablis or other white Burgundy.

<u>Foods that Pair Well with Chardonnay Wines</u>
This is a wine that adapts well.
Aged Chardonnay: Shellfish and other seafood, pork and veal, chicken with white sauce, pasta with white sauce.
Young Chardonnay: Shellfish, smoked meat, plain pasta, vegetarian dishes, cheese, omelets.

Chenin Blanc

Description

A high-acid grape that makes wines typically dry, but occasionally somewhat sweet. Often used as a blend (mixed with other grapes to make wine). Flavors may be of honey, fruits, or flowers when this wine is aged. The wine can be soft, even a bit spritzy.

Native Country

France (Loire). May be labeled Vouvray or Anjou

Foods That Pair Well with Chenin Blanc Wines

Seafood (shrimp, grilled fish, and fish with white sauces), pork, veal, chicken, quiche, pâté, vegetables, egg dishes, asparagus, fruit. Great for picnics.

Gewürztraminer

Description.

Grape with a spicy, perfume-like aroma that is easily recognizable. A versatile wine. Can make a dry or sweet wine and a dessert wine. Produces full-bodied wines with a color darker than most white wines. Can be a young wine or one with aging. California and Germany make sweeter wines than the Alsace area of France. These wines may taste flowery (like roses).

Native Countries

France (Alsace) and Germany

Foods That Pair Well with Gewürztraminer Wines
Smoked fish, stone crabs with mustard sauce, turkey, Oriental foods, spicy or hot foods, curry, sauerkraut, fruit.

Muscadet
(Called also Melon de Bourgogne or just Melon).
Description
A mild grape that produces dry wines of high acid with mild flavors. A quiet, gentle wine.

Native Country
France (Loire Valley)

Foods That Pair Well with Muscadet Wines
Shellfish, especially oysters.

Pinot Blanc
Description
A high-acid, mellow grape, lacks the aroma of some Alsatian grapes. Produces a light, crisp, dry wine, meant to be consumed young.

Native Country
France (Alsace and Burgundy)

Foods That Pair Well with Pinot Blanc Wines
Shellfish (especially oysters and shrimp), light chicken dishes, paté.

Pinot Gris

Description

A grape that creates fresh, soft wines. Also a dry, spicy, aromatic wine with honey flavors.

Native Country

Famous in France (in Alsace, called Tokay); Italy (known as Pinot Grigio)

Foods That Pair Well with Pinot Gris Wines

Plain fish, plain pasta, quiche, salads, melons.

Riesling

Description

This grape, like Chardonnay, is one of the world's most famous white grapes. Its aromatic wines are pale in color. Can make wines for long aging or to be consumed young. Can taste flowery, or have flavors of honey or green apples. These wines can be acid or sweet, but some are made into dry wines. Produces luscious dessert wines (late harvest). The name Riesling in generic form is copied all over the world, although the wines often taste nothing like the true German Johannisberg Riesling.

Native Countries

Germany and France (Alsace)

Foods That Pair Well with Riesling Wines

Seafood, ham, poultry, soft and/or mild cheeses, quiche, fruits. A good sipping wine.

Lighter Rieslings are good with smoked fish, pizza, egg dishes, Indian foods, Mexican foods. Drier Rieslings are good with spicy, hot foods, mild sausages. Pair sweeter Riesling wines with desserts.

Sauvignon Blanc
<u>Description</u>

A grape high in acid. Sometimes this grape makes sharp, zesty wines with fresh flavors, and wines with flavors of herbs or grass. When combined with the Sémillon grape, the wines will be smoother and without grassy flavors. May be made into a wine for aging. Often called Fumé Blanc wine. In Australia, this grape combined with Sémillon creates a more full-bodied wine than in France.

<u>Native Country</u>

France: Loire Valley region, called Pouilly-Fumé; Graves region, sometimes blended with Sémillon for Sauternes (sweet dessert wine), but unblended and/or blended for a dry wine

<u>Foods That Pair Well with Sauvignon Blanc Wines</u>

Light fish dishes and grilled fish, shellfish, light veal and pork dishes, poultry, pasta, curried dishes, spicy foods with the grassy wines, vegetables, foods with white cream sauces, Oriental foods. When blended into a Sauterne, usually pairs with desserts.

Sémillon
Description
This golden grape by itself does not make a particularly popular wine, but blended with Sauvignon Blanc, ah! what smooth wines. These grapes produce sweet wines (Sauternes) or dry wines (Graves). Sémillon has many flavors. It is blended also with Chardonnay in some countries (called sem/chard). In Australia, this grape is called Hunter Riesling. A good sipping wine.

Native Country
France: blended with Sauvignon Blanc for Sauternes and Graves

Foods That Pair Well with Sémillon Wines
Same foods as Sauvignon Blanc when combined with that grape. Otherwise do well with chicken dishes with white sauces, light meat dishes, light pastas, vegetables.

Trebbiano and Garganega
Description
These grapes make light, dry wines to be consumed young. The wines lack the variety of flavors of many other white wines, although the Soave Classico wines sometimes have an almond flavor. A good sipping wine. Chardonnay and Pinot Blanc are now blended with these grapes to make Soave.

Native Country
Italy (Soave)

Light foods, such as plain seafood, poultry, light pasta, vegetables, Caesar salad.

Red Grapes

Cabernet Sauvignon
Description
This grape makes dry wines with tannin and majestic complexity, the most popular, powerful wines in the world. These grapes are frequently blended with other grapes to soften the wines.

Some wines are produced for aging and taste bitter when young. When these wines are aged, they have flavors of oak, vanilla, and dark berry fruits. Most Cabernet Sauvignon wines, however, are meant to be consumed young. This grape is grown all over the world.

Native Country
France (Bordeaux)

Foods That Pair Well with Cabernet Sauvignon Wines
Lamb, beef, game, pork and veal, meat stews, casseroles, nuts, cheddar and other strong cheeses, some fruits, chocolate.

Corvina
Description
This grape is blended with Rondinella and Molinara to create light, simple wines, usually soft.

Can be fruity, and with an almond flavor.

Native Country

In Italy, makes Bardolino and Valpolicella. Valpolicella is the fuller-bodied wine.

Foods That Pair Well with These Wines

Meat loaf, pork and veal, lamb dishes, pasta with cream sauce, eggplant, picnic foods.

Gamay
Description

This grape makes wines with a fruity aroma. Produces light or medium-bodied wines with low tannin. These red wines welcome chilling and are great for picnics in hot weather.

Native Country

France (Beaujolais). In the United States there are Napa Gamay and Gamay Beaujolais grapes which make wines similar to the Gamay wines from France; both are fruity, light or medium-bodied wines.

Foods That Pair Well with Gamay Wines

Pork and veal, ham, rich sauce chicken dishes, poultry, hamburgers, meat loaf, pizza, pasta. Suitable for many foods and for picnics.

Grenache
Description

A scented, sweet grape that makes wines that are fruity and low in tannin. The grapes are often blended for creating different wine styles including robust or lighter rosé.

Native Countries

Spain (Rioja), where it is called Garnacha (sometimes blended with Tempranillo), and France (Rhône)

Foods That Pair Well with Grenache Wines

Salmon and other seafood, rich sauce poultry dishes, lamb, ham, beef, casseroles, sausage, stews, pork chops and ribs, flavorful cheeses.

Lambrusco
Description

A grape that makes light-bodied wines with a bit of spritz, a dry wine or a wine with a bit of sweetness. To be consumed when young.

Native Country

In Italy, makes the famous Lambrusco wines

Foods That Pair Well with Lambrusco Wines

Light dishes such as plain pasta. Good sipping wine.

Merlot
Description

This grape produces dry, mellow, fruity, delicate wines with less tannin than Cabernet Sauvignon and a bit softer. It creates many styles of wine.

Whereas the Merlot grape has traditionally been used for blending, especially with Cabernet

Sauvignon, wines now made from this grape, and called Merlot, have become popular.

<u>*Native Country*</u>
In France, blended with Cabernet Sauvignon for Bordeaux wines

<u>*Foods That Pair Well with Merlot Wines*</u>
Rich sauce fish and poultry dishes, stew, lamb, beef and corned beef, ham, ribs, roast chicken, grilled vegetables.

Nebbiolo and Barbera
<u>Description</u>
Nebbiolo is a high-tannin, high-acid grape. Barbera is a high-acid grape with less tannin than Nebbiolo. Both of these grapes make light-bodied wines or full-bodied wines for aging. The Nebbiolo grape makes the lighter wine.

<u>*Native Country*</u>
In Italy, Barbera makes Barbera wines. Nebbiolo makes Barolo, Barbaresco, and Gattinara wines.

<u>*Foods That Pair Well with These Wines*</u>
Pork and veal, stews, game, casseroles, powerful cheeses.

Petite Sirah
<u>Description</u>
This high-acid grape produces dry, tart, spicy, powerful wines. The grape is a good blend with Zinfandel and other grapes.

<u>Native Country</u>

Unknown.Currently grown in California and South America

<u>Foods That Pair Well with Petite Sirah Wines</u>

Beef, stews, game such as pheasant and duck, strong cheeses.

Pinot Noir
<u>Description</u>

The grapes are elegant, fruity, and earthy. They can make delicate or full-bodied wines in many styles and qualities. The grapes produce a softer, fruitier wine than Cabernet Sauvignon. Also used for Blanc de Noir Champagne.

<u>Native Country</u>

France (Burgundy and Champagne regions)

<u>Foods That Pair Well with Pinot Noir Wines or Burgundy Wines</u>

Strong-flavored shellfish, grilled salmon, tuna, lamb, white meat with red or rich sauces, barbecued game such as pheasant and duck, ham, omelets, Brie, and other mild cheeses.

Sangiovese
<u>Description</u>

This high-acid grape creates excellent wines with a little zest, as well as different qualities and styles of wine. Blended with other grapes for Chianti. Creates a dry, medium-bodied, or powerful wine.

Native Country
   In Italy (Tuscany) creates Brunello di Montalcino and is blended with other grapes for Chianti and Vino Nobile di Montepulciano.

Foods That Pair Well with Sangiovese Wines
   Beef, game, stews, chicken, barbecued meats, pizza, heavy pasta.

Syrah (Shiraz)
Description
   This grape makes fruity, dry, dark, full-bodied wines. It can produce a wine for long aging. In Australia, the grape is known as Shiraz.

Native Country
   In France (Rhône) makes Hermitage and Côte Rôtie.

Foods That Pair Well with Syrah Wines
   Strong-flavored foods, game, spicy foods, beef, stews, lamb, barbecued foods, cheddar and other strong cheeses.

Tempranillo
Description
   This low-acid, low-alcohol grape is blended with Garnacha and other grapes to produce smooth, full-bodied, often oaky, buttery-flavored wines.

Native Country
   Spain (Rioja)

Foods That Pair Well with Tempranillo Wines

Beef, sausage, roast chicken, pork, ham, flavorful cheeses.

Zinfandel
Description

This spicy grape makes many styles of wine: red, white, and blush; full-bodied, medium-bodied, and light; spicy, sweet, crisp, or dry with tannin. Some of the red wines are made for long aging. The blush wines are crisp, fresh, and with flavors of roses. A late harvest Zinfandel at a party is a guaranteed success. Warning: you'll have to search to locate this one, but you'll be glad you did.

Native Country

This grape is popular on the West Coast of the United States, but is thought to originate in Italy

Foods That Pair Well with Zinfandel Wines

With full-bodied wines—sausage, pork, veal, spareribs, game, hamburgers, roasts, steak, smoked meats, chili, many cheeses.

With blush and lighter wines—Ham, turkey, poultry, cold cuts, spicy foods, chef salad, picnic foods.

Fortifed Wines
Description

Wines that have an added neutral spirit, such as brandy. High in alcohol. These wines include Ports, Sherries, Madeiras.

Foods That Pair Well with Fortified Wines
Apples, desserts, olives, nuts, cheese. Port is famous for its pairing with Stilton cheese.

Champagne and Sparkling Wines
Description
Wines with carbon dioxide trapped in the bottle, which gives the wine an effervescence.

Foods That Pair Well with Champagne and Sparkling Wines
Dry Champagnes go well with many foods, especially seafood (caviar, sushi), turkey, ham, pasta, fried foods, fruits, berries, eggs such as omelets, soups, vegetarian dishes, corn on the cob, tomato dishes, foie gras, salty cheeses, salty foods such as nuts. Remember that some Champagnes are dry and others sweet. Sweet Champagnes pair better with sweeter foods and desserts.

Sauternes and Dessert (Late Harvest) Wines
Description
Wines that are made from grapes picked after the normal harvest.

Foods That Pair Well with Sauternes and Dessert Wines
Fresh fruits, nuts, desserts

Chapter 5

Food with Wine

Experiment with food and wine. If you cannot taste a wine served with a particular food, or cannot taste a food served with a particular wine, the one lacking in flavor is not bold enough to stand up to the other (a light Italian Soave with a heavy beef dish). Certain foods and wines are well suited to one another (Port with Stilton cheese or Amontillado Sherry with nuts). Some wines contrast the characteristics of specific foods (Champagne and salty foods). Also, acid and tannin wines cut the fat in foods (a Cabernet or red Rioja wine served with a piece of fatty beef).

Try the same wine with and without food and then with a variety of foods, and ask yourself these questions:

- Is the wine more appealing before, during, or after a meal and why? (Some wines have an unpleasant tannin taste by themselves, but with foods such as beef may become softer and more palatable.)

- Do the subtle differences in the wine change as the wine temperature changes? (Some complex white wines have more flavor if they are not ice cold.)

- Does the wine taste better if the weather is cool or hot? (On some days, an ice cold glass of light wine hits the spot; on cooler days, around a fireplace, a red wine or fortified wine might be more appealing.)

- Experience will be your best teacher. Perhaps you won't notice all these variations and will wonder what all the commotion is about. Perhaps you won't enjoy a particular wine at all. Judge the wine for yourself.

These are some current guidelines for serving foods and wines which wine and food lovers find helpful.

- Sweet food (sweet wine, full-bodied wine)
- Strong sauce (strong wine)
- Rich dish (full-bodied wine)
- Light dish (light wine)
- Acid dish (dry wine)
- Fatty food (acid, full-bodied wine, or sparkling wine)
- Heavy, aged cheese (full-bodied, powerful wine)
- Cream cheese (Sparking wine, Champagne or Chardonnay)
- Light cheese (light wine)

If you are serving several wines and want to be

formal, the suggested sequence is as follows:

- Dry, then sweet (Cabernet Sauvignon, then Sauternes)
- Light bodied, then full bodied (Beaujolais, then Classico Chianti)
- White, then red (Chardonnay, then Côtes-du-Rhône)
- Plain, then fine (Chenin Blanc, then French Chablis)
- Young, then mature (Young Chardonnay, then Aged Chardonnay)

Food and Wine

FOOD WITH WINE

Suggested Wines

Food	Wine Style	Economical	Moderate
Vegetable dishes	Rosé, white Champagne, young Chardonnay, Sauvignon Blanc, Sémillon, light Italian	Great Western Sparkling (US)	Scharffenberger Sparkling (US)
Sauerkraut	Gewürztraminer	Fetzer Gewürztraminer (US)	Zind Humbrecht Gewürztraminer (Alsace, France)
Grilled or roasted vegetables	Merlot, light Italian reds, light Riojas	Montecillo Viña Cumbrero Red (Rioja, Spain)	La Rioja Alta S.A. Viña Alberdi Reserva (Rioja, Spain)
Salad	Italian whites, aged Chardonnay, dry Sauvignon Blanc	Orvieto Classico Ruffino (Italy)	Elena Walch Alto Adige Pinot Grigio (Italy)

Cheeses			
Mild	Young Chardonnay	Fetzer white Zinfandel (US)	Thomas Mitchell Marsanne (Australia)
Stilton	Port	Château Reynella Old Cave Tawny Port (Australia)	Fonseca Bin 27 Fine Reserve (Portugal)
Strong	Rioja, Grenache, Cabernet, Syrah (also called Shiraz), Nebbiolo, Zinfandel	Penfolds Koonunga Hill Shiraz/Cabernet (Australia)	Vietti Barbaresco (Italy)
Aromatic	Riesling or Gewürztraminer	Château Ste Michelle Johannisberg Riesling (US)	Weingut Gunderloch Riesling Spätlese (Germany)
Pasta	Chardonnay, Muscadet, Sauvignon Blanc, Pinot Grigio, Soave	Lindemans Chardonnay, or Sem/Char magnum (Australia)	Château St. Jean Chardonnay (US)
Pasta with a weighty sauce	Gamay, light Italian reds, Merlot	Réserve St Martin Merlot (*Vin de Pays d'Oc*, France)	Clos du Bois Merlot (US)
Pizza	Light red Italian wines, such as Chianti, Lambrusco, white Champagne, Gamay	Rocca delle Macie Chianti Classico (Italy)	Aziano Chianti Classico (Italy)

Food	Wine Style	Suggested Wines	
		Economical	*Moderate*
Seafood Shellfish	White Champagne, aged Chardonnay, Pinot Blanc, Muscadet, dry Sauvignon Blanc, dry Sémillon, Chenin Blanc	George Duboeuf Chardonnay (*Vin de Pays d'Oc*, France)	Chablis Lupé-Cholet (French)
Stone crabs with mustard sauce	Dry Riesling or dry Gewürztraminer	Rosemount Estate Traminer Riesling (Australia)	Alsace Cuvée Les Amours "Hugel" Pinot Blanc (France)
Tuna	Pinot Noir, Chardonnay, Grenache, Merlot	Lindemans Merlot (Australia)	Kendall-Jackson Pinot Noir (US)
Baked or broiled	Rosé, white Champagne, Chardonnay, Pinot Grigio, dry Sauvignon Blanc	Robert Mondavi Rosé (US)	Château Souverain Chardonnay (US)
Chicken Plain sauce	Rosé and light reds, white Champagne, Chardonnay, Sauvignon Blanc, Sémillon, Riesling, Chenin Blanc	Rosemount Estate Sémillon Chardonnay (Australia)	Frog's Leap Sauvignon Blanc (US)

Weighty sauce	Gamay, Grenache, Sauvignon Blanc, Merlot, full-bodied Chardonnay, Rhône	Fortant de France Merlot (*Vin de Pays d'Oc*, France)	Château de Cros Blanc de Sauvignon (Bordeaux, France)
Grilled or roasted	Beaujolais, Rosé, Sauvignon Blanc, Red Zinfandel	Rosemount Estate Shiraz/Cabernet (Australia)	Burgess Zinfandel (US)
Turkey	White Champagne, Rosé, Chardonnay, Gewürztraminer, Riesling, Sauvignon Blanc, Sémillon, Gamay, Pinot Noir	George Duboeuf Beaujolais-Villages (France)	Trénel Moulin-à-Vent Beaujolais (France)
Other fowl	Rosé, white Champagne, Pinot Noir, Grenache, Gamay, Valpolicella, Chianti	Louis Jadot Beaujolais-Villages (France)	Rocche Dei Manzoni Vigna Matinera Dolcetto d'Alba (Italy)
Beef and lamb Weighty dishes	Cabernet Sauvignon, Rioja, Zinfandel, Barolo, Grenache	Lindemans Shiraz (Australia)	Château la Boisserie St-Emilion Grand Cru (France)
Lighter dishes	Gamay, Bardolino, Grenache, Valpolicella, Merlot, Chianti, Petite Sirah, Pinot Noir, Nebbiolo	L'Orval Merlot (*Vin de Pays d'Oc*, France)	Gallo Sonoma Merlot (US)

Food	Wine Style	Suggested Wines	
		Economical	*Moderate*
Pork and veal Plain	Rosé, Chardonnay, Muscadet, Sauvignon Blanc, Riesling	L'Orval Chardonnay (*Vin de Pays d'Oc*, France)	Clos du Bois Chardonnay (US)
Weighty dishes	Aged Chardonnay, Cabernet Sauvignon, Zinfandel, Gamay, Rioja, Valpolicella, Barbera, Nebbiclo	George Duboeuf Cabernet Sauvignon (*Vin de Pays d'Oc*, France)	De Loach Cabernet Sauvignon (US)
Ham	Rosé, white Champagne, Riesling, Merlot, Gamay, Pinot Noir, Chenin Blanc	Mondavi White Zinfandel magnum (US)	Domaine de Longval Tavel (Rhône, France)
Sausage	Grenache, dry Zinfandel, Riesling, Gewürztraminer, Shiraz, Pinot Noir	Fortant de France Syrah (*Vin de Pays d'Oc*, France)	Rosemount Estate Shiraz (Australia)
Game	Cabernet Sauvignon, Chianti, Nebbiclo, Barbera, Grenache Syrah (Shiraz), Zinfandel	Réserve St Martin Cabernet (*Vin de Pays d'Oc*, France)	Rabbit Ridge Zinfandel (US)

Food	Wine types	Suggested wine	Suggested wine
Oriental	White Champagne, Riesling, Gewürztraminer	Since there are so many interesting flavors and spices associated with Oriental foods, the restaurant server may be of help to you. Tott's Brut (US)	Domaine Chandon Brut Cuvée (US)
Nuts	Cabernet Sauvignon, Champagne, Dessert wines	George Duboeuf Cabernet Sauvignon (*Vin de Pays d'Oc*, France)	Blandy's Malmsey Madeira (Portugal)
Eggs	White Champagne, young Chardonnay, Riesling, Chenin Blanc	Fortant de France Chardonnay (*Vin de Pays d'Oc*, France)	Bollinger Special Cuvée Brut (Champagne, France)
Spicy foods	Sauvignon blanc, Grenache, Gewürztraminer, red or white Zinfandel, Syrah (Shiraz)	L'Orval Syrah (*Vin de Pays d'Oc*, France)	Quivira Zinfandel (US)
Picnics	Almost anything, including the non-breakable boxes of wine	August Sebastiani Heritage Merlot magnum (US)	George Duboeuf Morgon Beaujolais (France)
Meat sandwiches	Grenache, Valpolicella, Merlot, Bardolino, Gamay, Lambrusco	L'Orval Merlot (*Vin de Pays d'Oc*, France)	Secco-Bertani Valpolicella-Valpantena (Italy)

Food	Wine Style	Suggested Wines	
		Economical	*Moderate*
Fried foods	Champagne, Chianti	Codorníu (Spain)	Roederer Estate Brut (US)
Desserts			
Chocolate	Cabernet Sauvignon, Port	Clocktower Tawny Port (Australia)	Sandeman Founders Reserve Port (Portugal)
Sweet Desserts	Sweet or semi-sweet Champagne, Sauternes, sweet Riesling	Clos Ste Magdeleine Cassis (Sauternes, France)	Château Coutet à Barsac (Barsac, France)
Fruits	Sweet or semi-sweet Champagne, Muscadet, sweet Gewürztraminer, Chenin Blanc, Sauterne, sweet Riesling	Tott's Blanc de Noir Sparkling (US)	Domaine de Durban Muscat de Beaumes-de-Venise (France)

How to Say It: The Wine-Lover's Guide to Pronunciation

Amontillado   ah mon tee yah' doe
Anjou   ahn joo'
Auslese   ow' slay seh
Barbaresco   bar bah ress' coe
Barbera   bar ber' ah
Bardolino   bar-doe-lee'noe
Barolo   bah roh' loe
Barsac   bar' sac
Beaujolais   boh ju lay'
Beaune   bone
Beerenauslese   beer en ow' slay seh
Blanc de Blanc   blahnc' duh blahnc'
Blanc de Noir   blahnc duh nwar'
Blanc Fumé   blahnc foo may'
Bodega   bo day' ga
Bordeaux   bore doe'
Brouilly   brew yee'
Brunello di Montalcino   brew nell' oh dee mon-tahl chee' noe
Brut   brute
Cabernet Sauvignon   ca ber nay' so vin yawn'
Cassis   cah seece'
Cave   cahv
Chablis   shah blee'
Chardonnay   shar doe nay'

Châteauneuf-du-Pape   shah toe nuf' dew pahp'
Chenin Blanc   shen' nin blahnc
Corvina   core vea' nah
Côte de Beaune   coat duh bone'
Côte Chalonnaise   coat shah-lo-nay'
Côte de Nuits   coat duh nwee
Côte d'Or   coat door'
Côtes du Rhône   coat dew roan'
Côte Rôtie   coat ro tee'
Crémant   cray mahn'
Cru   crew
Cuvée   coo vay'
Dolcetto   dole chet' toe
Entre-Deux-Mers   ahn' truh duh mare'
Fiaschi   fee ahss' kee
Fino   fee' no
Gamay   gamm aye'
Garanega   gahr ga neh' gah
Gewürztraminer   gah vertz' trah mee' ner
Graves   grahv
Grenache   gre nash'
Hermitage   ahr' me tajh
Johannisberg   yo hahn' iss burg
Lambrusco   lam broo' scoh
Liebfraumilch   leeb' frow milsch
Mâcon   mah' kahn
Médoc   may' dawc
Merlot   mer loe'
Mersault   mer sew'
Mosel-Saar-Ruwer   moh zel zahr rew' ver
Müller-Thurgau   mule' er thur' gow
Muscadet   moos ka day'
Nebbiolo   neh be oh' loe
Nouveau   new voe'
Petite Syrah   peh teet' see rah'
Phylloxera   fi lox' eh rah
Pinot Blanc   pea' no blahnc
Pinot Grigio   pea' no gree' djoh

Pinot Gris   pea' no gree'
Pinot Noir   pea' no nwar
Pomerol   pom ah roll'
Pouilly-Fuissé   poo' yee fwee say'
Pouilly-Fumé   poo' yee foo may'
Premier Cru   preem' yea crew
Retsina   rett see' nah
Rheingau   rhine' gow
Rheinhessen   rhine' hessen
Rheinpfalz   rhine' faltz
Riesling   rees' ling
Rioja   ree oh' ha
Sancerre   sahn sare'
Sangiovese   san joh vey' zeh
Sauternes   saw turn'
Sauvignon Blanc   so' vin yawn blahnc
Sekt   sekt
Sémillon   seh' mee yahn
Shiraz   shi' roz
Soave   swa' vay
Solera   sew lair' ah
Sommelier   sew mah yeah'
Spätlese   shpate' lay zeh
Sylvaner   sil voh' ner
Syrah   see rah'
Tavel   ta vel'
Tempranillo   tem pra ni' yoh
Trebbiano   treb yon' noh
Trockenbeerenauslese   troch' en bear en ow' slay seh
Valpolicella   val poh lee chell' ah
Vouvray   voo vray'
Zinfandel   zin' van del

Wine-Lover's Glossary of Names and Terms

Acidity
   Natural wine ingredient, giving the wine a tartness.
Alcohol
   Created by the fermentation process of the grapes. The content in wine may vary from 7 to 20%.
Amontillado
   A nutty flavored sherry.
Amphora
   A container made of pottery used in the Mediterranean area in ancient times.
Apéritif
   Beverage taken before a meal.
Appellation d'Origine Contrôlée (AOC)
   The finest quality of French wines, a term found on the bottle label.
Aroma
   The scent of grapes in a young wine.
Aromatic
   A wine full of rich scent and flavor.
Auslese
   A QmP category, German wine, made from late harvest grapes.
Beerenauslese
   A QmP category, German sweet wine.
Blanc de Blanc
   White wine made from white grapes.
Blanc de Noir
   White or pale pink wine made from Pinot Noir grapes or other red grapes.
Bodega
   Spanish winery.
Body
   Texture and/or weight of a wine.

Botrytis Cinerea

A mold that can enhance the flavor of certain sweet wines.

Bouquet

Wine aroma, not the grapey smells.

Breathing

Allowing wine to be exposed to the air before drinking.

Brut

Dry Champagne and Sparkling wine - drier than an extra-dry wine.

Carafe

A restaurant house wine served in an open container.

Chablis

1) A wine made from the Chardonnay grape in the Chablis region of France.

2) An American generic term for certain inexpensive white wines.

Chaptalization

Adding sugar to the grape juice at or before fermentation.

Château

French winery.

Claret

British term for red Bordeaux wine.

Cognac

A brandy from the Cognac area of France.

Complex wine

A wine that has been barrel-aged, with diversified and balanced flavors.

Corked

A spoiled wine, with a musty odor and taste.

Crisp

A fresh and lively wine, usually white.

Cru

Growth, in French, referring to a vineyard and its ranking

Cuvée
A specific blend or vat of wine.

Decanting
Pouring of a wine into another container, to allow it to breathe or to remove it from its sediment.

Demi-Sec
A sweet Champagne or sparkling wine; sweeter than a sec wine.

Denominazione di Origine Controllata (DOC)
The body that governs the quality of Italy's wines.

Denominazione di Origine Controllata e Garantita (DOCG)
Italy's highest ranking quality wines.

Doux
A very sweet Champagne - sweeter than a demi-sec.

Dry
A wine that is not sweet, without sugar.

Effervescent
A bubbly wine, as carbon dioxide gas escapes after the wine bottle is opened.

Eiswein
A German sweet wine, made from grapes allowed to freeze before harvesting.

Enology (also oenology)
The science and study of the making of wine.

Fermentation
The process whereby grapes (with yeasts and sugar) are converted into wine.

Fino
A very dry Sherry.

Flute
1) Tall, thin glass with a stem, used for Champagne.
2) Tall, thin bottle used for German wines.

Fortified
A high-alcohol wine, made by adding a brandy to the wine.

Full-Bodied
Wines that feel weighty in the mouth.

Generic

U.S. inexpensive wines named after a French regional wine, such as Burgundy, Chablis, Sherry.

Halbtrocken

A German word for semi-dry.

Hectare

A term measuring land area in countries that use the metric system (1 acre = 2/5 hectare).

Herbaceous

A wine with fresh, herb-like aroma and flavors.

House Wine

A wine selected by a restaurant, often a jug wine, for an inexpensive price.

Hybrid Grape

A cross between two or more grape varieties.

Jug Wine

Inexpensive wines often sold in large bottles.

Kabinett

A German wine of above average quality, but the lowest of the QmP wines.

Labrusca

Name for many American grape varieties, of the *Vitis labrusca* species (Concord, Catawba).

Landwein

German table wine—better than a Tafelwein.

Late Harvest Wine

A very sweet wine made from late-harvested grapes.

Lees

The grape sediment created as juice ferments and matures.

Legs

Little streams of wine that coat and run down the inside of the glass after we swirl or sip the wine.

Light-Bodied

A delicate-flavored wine (low in grape extracts and alcohol).

Madeira

A sweet fortified wine from Madeira, Portugal.

Magnum

A large bottle of wine, twice the size of a standard bottle.

Medium-Bodied

A wine that is between a light-bodied and a full-bodied texture.

Méthode Champenoise

The French term denoting their Champagne-making process.

Mis en Bouteille

French for "bottled."

Mis en Bouteille au Château

French for made and bottled at the Château (winery).

Must

Grape juice to be made into wine.

Négociant

A French term denoting a wine shipper/wholesaler.

Nose

The fragrance of a wine (combination of aroma and bouquet).

Nouveau

New, as in Beaujolais Nouveau.

Oaky

The taste and smell of oak and toast in a wine.

Oloroso

Oxidized Sherries, sometimes sweet - such as Cream Sherries.

Organic Wine

A wine made without fertilizers or pesticides.

Phylloxera

A grape vine insect that can destroy the roots of the vines.

Port

A sweet fortified wine from Portugal.

Proprietary Name

Name given and marketed by a winemaker to denote a specific wine.

Qualitätswein mit Prädikat (QmP)
>The highest quality of German wine.

Reserve
>A U.S. wine label term, usually, but not always, meaning a wine of better quality.

Robust
>A wine with more texture than even a full-bodied wine.

Sauternes
>A sweet white Bordeaux wine.

Sec
>A semi-dry Champagne or Sparkling wine.

Sherry
>A sweet fortified wine from southern Spain.

Sipping Wine
>One that is pleasant to drink without food.

Soft Wine
>A wine that feels well balanced in the mouth, without harsh flavors or astringency.

Solera
>A way of blending certain wines to keep the wine styles consistent year after year.

Sommelier
>A specialized server in a restaurant who is familiar with wines.

Sparkling Wine
>A wine made bubbly by carbon dioxide gas trapped in the bottle.

Spätlese
>A sweet German QmP wine, made from overly ripe grapes.

Spritzer
>A drink of club soda and white wine over ice.

Spumante
>Sparkling wine from Italy.

Still Wine
>A non-effervescent wine.

Sulfites
> Sulfurous acid salts, a natural ingredient of wine, stemming from the fermentation process, but also used to sterilize, as an insecticide, and to prevent spoilage.

Sweet Wine
> A wine high in sugar content.

Table Wine
> A non-fortified, non-sparkling wine. In the U.S. a wine with an alcohol level between 7% to 14%.

Tafelwein
> The lowest category of QmP German wine—a table wine.

Tannin
> Found in the stems and pulp of grapes, this substance causes the puckering sensation in the mouth.

Tawny
> A form of Port, tawny in color, usually less expensive than vintage Ports.

Trocken
> German term for dry.

Trockenbeerenauslese
> The highest quality of QmP German wine, expensive, very sweet and low in alcohol.

Varietal
> Referring to a grape variety from which a wine is predominantly made.

Vin Délimité de Qualité Supérieure (VDQS)
> The second highest quality of French wine.

Vin de Pays
> A quality category of French wine, higher than *Vin de Table* but lower than *Appellation Contrôlée* or *Vin Supérieure*.

Vintage
> Year of grape harvest, often found on the bottle label.

Woody
> A wine with the flavor of wood (from barrel aging).

If You Want to Know More...

Adams, Leon D. *The Commonsense Book of Wine*, rev. San Francisco, CA.: The Wine Appreciation Guild, 1991.

Bespaloff, Alexis. *Alexis Bespaloff's Complete Guide to Wine* (rev). New York: Signet/Penguin Books,1994.

Clarke, Oz. *The Essential Wine Book,* rev. New York: Fireside/Simon & Schuster, 1988.

de Blij, Harm Jan. *Wine—A Geographic Appreciation.* Towota, New Jersey: Rowman & Allanheld, 1983.

Johnson, Hugh. *The World Atlas of Wine*, 4th ed., rev. New York: Simon & Schuster, 1994.

Masline, Shelagh Ryan. *The Concise Wine Guide.* New York: A Berkley Book/published by arrangement with The Philip Lief Group, 1993.

Perdue, Lewis. *The French Paradox and Beyond.* Sonoma, CA: Renaissance Publishing, 1992.

Robinson, Jancis. *Vines, Grapes and Wines.* New York: Alfred A. Knopf, 1986.

Robinson, Jancis, ed. *The Oxford Companion to Wine.* New York: Oxford Univeristy Press, 1994.

Waugh, Alec and the Editors of Time-Life Books. *Wines and Spirits,* rev. Alexandria: Time-Life Books, 1977.

Zraly, Kevin. *Windows of the World Complete Wine Course*, rev. New York: Sterling Publishing Company, 1993.

How to Order Additional Copies of
The Wine Lover's Question & Answer Book

Have copies of this book sent to yourself or to the
person of your choice.

Send $12.00 plus
$3.50 shipping to:

OAK BARREL PRESS
8770 Sunset Drive
Suite 262
Miami, Florida 33173

or call:

(305) 595-3246